LONDON DOORS

OLDCASTLE BOOKS

LONDON DOORS

CHARLES VINEY

1989

Oldcastle Books
18 Coleswood Road
Harpenden
Herts AL5 1EQ

British Library Cataloguing in Publication Data
Viney, *1954-*
        London doors,
        1, Great Britain. Doors
        I, Title
        721' .822'0941
        ISBN 0-948353-57-0

9 8 7 6 5 4 3 2 1

For Becky with Love

INTRODUCTION

Front doors, as the focus of any facade, represent the most important visual aspect of the exterior of a house. They are not only vitally important in establishing the character of the principal front; additionally, they provide an invaluable guide to the wealth, status and pretension of the house owner. As a result, there exists more variety in the form and decoration of the front door and its surround than can be witnessed in any other external architectural feature.

This book is a celebration of this variety. It represents an indispensable source for doors both grand and humble, elaborate and austere. And as the past arbiter of national taste, exercising far more direct influence on architectural fashions than comparable capitals such as Paris or Madrid, London naturally possesses the greatest diversity of doors and doorcases in the country. Admittedly few examples from the Medieval, Tudor and Early Stuart periods survive in the capital - the Great Fire of 1666 and the subsequent surge of speculative housing development saw to that. Essentially, then, this pictorial analysis of London's doors is a history of the Georgian panelled door and its 19th and 20th century descendants. Within these parameters one can find the spectacular array of designs and colours depicted in the following pages.

The standard Medieval door comprised interlinked planks bound together with horizontal ledges and prominent, decorated hinges. By 1700, however, the more sophisticated and complex panelled door had become the norm. It consisted of an 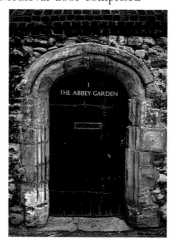 arrangement of stiles and rails - respectively, the vertical and horizontal external members - surrounding a symmetrical arrangement of flat panels. The panels were often 'fielded', that is, raised to be either flush with, or slightly more depressed than, the rails; in most 18th century doors these panels were also provided with moulded edges, to link them more effectively with the rest of the composition.

The most common Early Georgian form was the six-panelled door. This type features in a large number of the following views, including that of what must be the most fam-ous front door in the world - Number 10, Downing St. Westminster. Frequently, the bottom two panels were flush with the bottom stile, and provided merely with a single mould-ing linking them directly to the rails,

in contrast to the more individually fielded upper panels; this was to give greater strength to the part of the door which received the most punishment - generally from impatient feet. Note, too, that the top two panels of Georgian doors were never square - a dis-position found in most of today's sham, pseudo-Georgian products - but were decidedly rectangular, and laid horizontally. Palladian door panels, like much else in the Palladian house of the middle decades

of the 18th century, tended to follow strict rules of proportion, rules that were intended to replicate as far as possible the 'perfect' architecture of Ancient Greece and Rome.

The grandest doors of the Georgian era were generally made from seasoned oak or West Indian mahogany. In less wealthy houses, however, inferior oak or softwoods were used, and invariably painted either a single, dark colour or (particularly in the early 18th century and Regency periods) 'grained' in imitation of expensive woods. Whilst the body of the Georgian door was usually quite plain, with sober and unob-trusive mouldings, great exuberance was shown in the form of the adjacent doorcase

and related fanlight. Early 18th century
doorcases
generally took
the form of
columns or
pilasters
supporting
elaborate hoods,
flat cornices,
pediments or
projecting
canopies. The
more ostentat–
ious the door–
case, the
more successful
the house was as
an advertisement for the owner's wealth and
taste. From c.1720 onwards the characteristic
'temple front' Palladian doorcase began to
accomodate a
glass fanlight
with wooden
glazing bars
above the door.
Fanlights were
probably orig–
inally derived
from round-
headed sash
windows, and
allowed light to
penetrate into
the internal
hallway for the
first time.
Early Palladian examples include the common
pattern of thick, tapering glazing bars radiat-
ing from the centre, as seen at 10 Downing
Street; gradually, however, the design of
fanlights became increasingly elaborate, particularly following the introduction of slim,
iron glazing bars in the mid-18th century. The
culmination of fanlight development came
in the last thirty years of the century, when
Adam-style fanlights with profuse and delicate
tracery came to dominate the doorway.
   18th century
door furniture
was simple and
usually made
from wrought
iron, painted
black, blue or
lead-colour.
Brass com-
pounds only
began to be
widely employed
at the end of
the century,
and then brass
fittings were
only applied to grand doors. Door knobs were
often fluted, and placed at waist height, at the

intersection of the muntin - the central stile - and the lock rail. The characteristic Regency 'lion's head' door knocker first appeared in c.1800. Locks remained fairly primitive until the mid-19th century, when the rotating Yale lock (patented in 1848), able to detect the tiny variations in key patterns, became widespread. Bell-pulls, however, were much in evidence as early as 1800, and on the exterior usually took the form of a small brass knob inset in a circular panel, placed to the side of the doorcase.

The standard Regency or early 19th century door had fewer panels than its 18th century predecessors - usually two or possibly three, often with rounded corners. Doorcases had become much less complex, and were often mere reeded jambs supporting a flat entablature. Fanlights, too, had grown less elaborate since the days of Robert Adam, and had almost disappeared by the 1840's. By the mid-19th century glass was for the first time beginning to appear *within* the body of the door - originally in place of the two upper panels, and later all of the panels in certain examples being  replaced by two vertical panes. These developments were facilitated by the great advances being made in glass technology; in 1832, for example, Lucas Chance introduced continental - style plate glass into Britain, enabling the production of far larger pane areas. The increasing sophistication and reliability of 19th century glass accordingly gave Victorian and Edwardian door designers endless possibilities in the fields of colour and decoration.

By 1900 London front doors were being manufactured in a huge variety of forms. Door furniture was becoming increasingly profuse, and on some occasions was threatening to take over the whole door; in  particular, a fashion for pseudo-historical details such as carriage lamps, giving the most modest suburban house a veneer of bogus historicism, became prevalent. Since 1840, of course, there had been another necessary item of door furniture to accommodate: the letter-box. This was best placed either lying horizontally in the centre of the lock rail or vertically in the muntin, at head height. The photographs in this book demonstrate the differing solutions used - with varying degrees of success - to solve this aesthetic problem.

The last great age of London door design came with the interwar period, when stylised motifs were combined with an imaginative use of plain or stained glass to produce the classic suburban door so often associated with the new Metroland estates of Northwest London. Alas, in recent times these doors seem to be particularly vulnerable to replacement by sham-Georgian examples. It has to be admitted that in design terms many off-the-peg modern products have done very little to enhance his-torical door-  ways. Unpainted doors, fabricated from garish tropical hardwoods and featuring such ahis-torical elements as 'bottle-glass' panes, slipped fanlights and shiny, over-dominant brass fit-tings, appear as ludicrous parodies of their Georgian and Victorian antecedents. Additionally, the post-Arts and Crafts fad for 'honesty' in materials has encouraged many house owners to strip their front doors of all paintwork, thus exposing inferior woods which were never intended to be seen. At the same time original door furniture and stained glass is frequently lost or broken, and replaced with crude modern approximations.

The last ten or fifteen years, however, have seen an enormous increase in the numbers of house owners who seek to restore their door-way - and the rest of their home - to some-thing resembling the intentions of the original designers. Examples of this heartening approach, where doors once more become the focus of a dignified and balanced facade, can be seen throughout this book. I very much hope that *London Doors* will serve as a design guide for those home owners who would like to see their house recover its former glory; at the same time, it will doubtless reassure others of the continuing delight to be found in this most individual of architectural forms.

Steven Parissien
The Georgian Group
April 1989

PLATES

WESTMINSTER ABBEY, 13th Century

Plate 1

WESTMINSTER ABBEY, 14th Century

Plate 2

WESTMINSTER ABBEY, 13th Century

Plate 1

WESTMINSTER ABBEY, 14th Century

Plate 2

WESTMINSTER *c.*1500

Plate 3

ST. PAULS CATHEDRAL, 1700

Plate 4

WESTMINSTER *c.* 1720

Plate 5

MARBLE HILL *c.*1730

Plate 6

MARBLE HILL *c.* 1730

Plate 7

WESTMINSTER *c.*1730

Plate 8

No.10, DOWNING STREET, WESTMINSTER *c.*1730

Plate 9

No.11, DOWNING STREET, WESTMINSTER *c.*1730

Plate 10

CHELSEA *c.*1730

Plate 11

SPITALFIELDS *c.* 1740

Plate 12

SPITALFIELDS *c.*1740

Plate 13

THE TEMPLE *c.*1740

Plate 14

WESTMINSTER *c.* 1740

Plate 15

WESTMINSTER *c.*1740

Plate 16

WESTMINSTER ABBEY *c.*1750

Plate 17

CHELSEA *c.*1750

Plate 18

WESTMINSTER *c.*1750

Plate 19

MAYFAIR *c.* 1750

Plate 20

WESTMINSTER *c.*1760

Plate 21

CHELSEA *c.*1760

Plate 22

SPITALFIELDS *c.*1760

Plate 23

CHELSEA *c.*1760

Plate 24

WESTMINSTER *c.*1770

Plate 25

CAMDEN *c.*1770

Plate 26

WESTMINSTER *c.*1770

Plate 27

WESTMINSTER *c.*1770

Plate 28

ISLINGTON *c.*1770

Plate 29

CANONBURY *c.*1780

Plate 30

KEW *c*.1790

Plate 31

CHELSEA *c.* 1800

Plate 32

CHELSEA *c.* 1800

Plate 33

ISLINGTON *c.*1800

Plate 34

WESTMINSTER *c.*1800

Plate 35

WHITECHAPEL *c.* 1800

Plate 36

BANK OF ENGLAND, THE CITY *c.*1800

Plate 37

HOLBORN *c.* 1810

Plate 38

WAPPING *c.*1810

Plate 39

BARNSBURY *c.*1820

Plate 40

BARNSBURY *c.*1820

Plate 41

BARNSBURY *c.*1820

Plate 42

BARNSBURY *c.*1820

Plate 43

BARNSBURY *c.*1820

Plate 44

ISLINGTON *c.* 1820

Plate 45

FINSBURY *c.*1820

Plate 46

BOW *c.*1830

Plate 47

BOW *c.*1830

Plate 48

SPITALFIELDS *c.*1830

Plate 49

BARNSBURY *c.* 1830

Plate 50

BELGRAVIA *c.*1830

Plate 51

KEW *c.*1840

Plate 52

WESTMINSTER *c.*1840

Plate 53

BARNSBURY *c.* 1840

Plate 54

THE HOUSE OF LORDS, WESTMINSTER, 1847

Plate 55

CHELSEA *c.* 1850

Plate 56

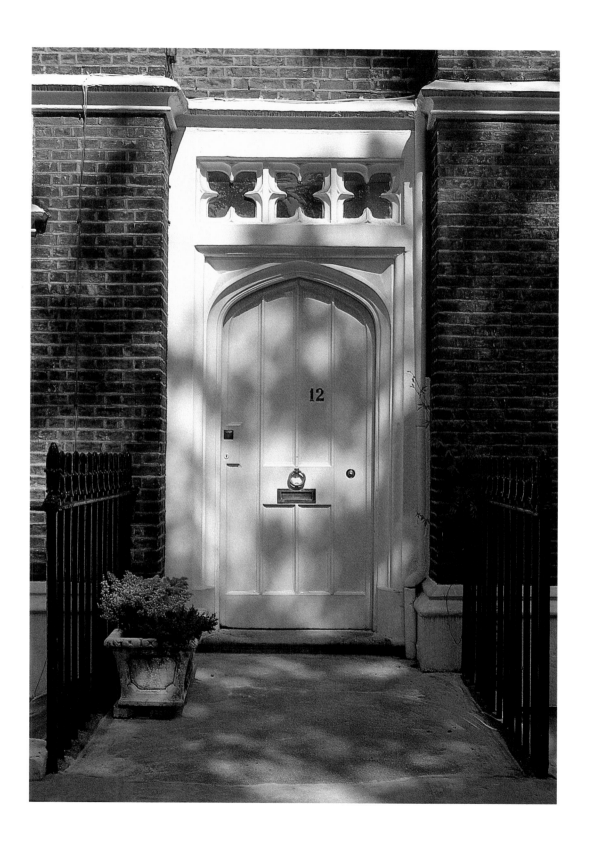

ISLINGTON *c.*1850

Plate 57

ISLINGTON *c.*1860

Plate 58

ROYAL AGRICULTURAL HALL, ISLINGTON, 1862

Plate 59

BROCKLEY *c.*1870

Plate 60

CHELSEA *c.*1875

Plate 61

TELEGRAPH HILL *c.* 1880

Plate 62

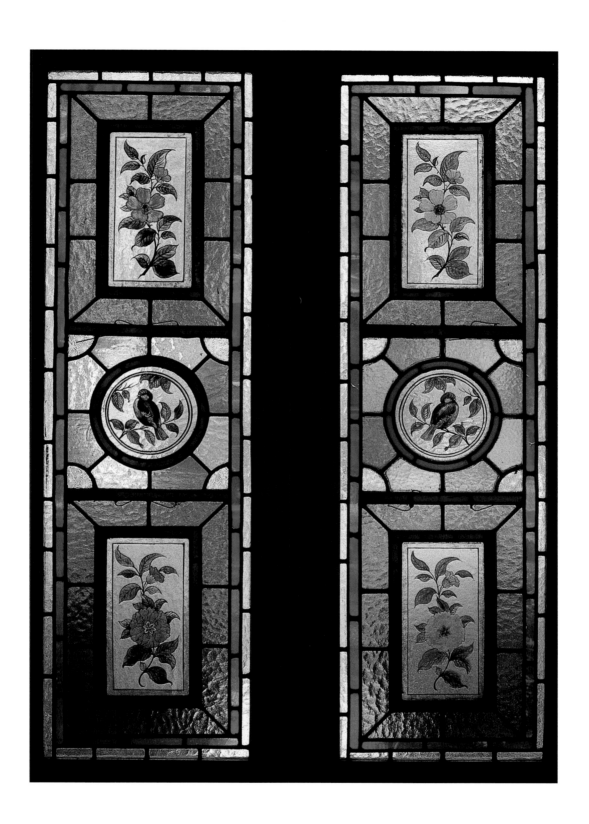

TELEGRAPH HILL, 1888

Plate 63

TELEGRAPH HILL, 1888

Plate 64

TELEGRAPH HILL, 1888

Plate 65

BELGRAVIA; ironwork *c.*1890

Plate 66

WESTMINSTER *c.*1900

Plate 67

MAYFAIR *c.* 1900

Plate 68

MAYFAIR *c.* 1900

Plate 69

CHELSEA *c.* 1910

Plate 70

PERIVALE *c.*1930

Plate 71

HOOVER BUILDING, PERIVALE, 1932

Plate 72

LIST OF PLATES